Douglas

by Jim Hewitson

LangSyne
PUBLISHING
WRITING *to* REMEMBER

LangSyne

PUBLISHING

WRITING *to* REMEMBER

Vineyard Business Centre,
Pathhead, Midlothian EH37 5XP
Tel: 01875 321 203 Fax: 01875 321 233
E-mail: info@lang-syne.co.uk
www.langsyneshop.co.uk

Design by Dorothy Meikle
Printed by Montgomery Litho, Glasgow
© Lang Syne Publishers Ltd 2011

ISBN 978-1-85217-066-0

Douglas

SEPT NAMES INCLUDE:

Agnew	Inglis
Blackett	Kilpatrick
Blackwood	Kirk
Breckenridge	Kirkland
Brown	Lockerby,
Caven	MacGuffey,
Dick	McKittrick
Dickey	Morton
Drysdale	Sandiland,
Foster	Symington
Glenn	Young

Douglas

MOTTO:
Jamais Arrière
(Never behind)

CREST:
A Salamander Encircled with Flames

Chapter one:

The origins of the clan system

by Rennie McOwan

The original Scottish clans of the Highlands and the great families of the Lowlands and Borders were gatherings of families, relatives, allies and neighbours for mutual protection against rivals or invaders.

Scotland experienced invasion from the Vikings, the Romans and English armies from the south. The Norman invasion of what is now England also had an influence on land-holding in Scotland. Some of these invaders stayed on and in time became 'Scottish'.

The word clan derives from the Gaelic language term 'clann', meaning children, and it was first used many centuries ago as communities were formed around tribal lands in glens and mountain fastnesses.

The format of clans changed over the centuries, but at its best the chief and his family held the land on behalf of all, like trustees, and the ordinary clansmen and women believed they had a blood relationship with the founder of their clan.

There were two way duties and obligations. An inadequate chief could be deposed and replaced by someone of greater ability.

Clan people had an immense pride in race. Their relationship with the chief was like adult children to a father and they had a real dignity.

The concept of clanship is very old and a more feudal notion of authority gradually crept in.

Pictland, for instance, was divided into seven principalities ruled by feudal leaders who were the strongest and most charismatic leaders of their particular groups.

By the sixth century the 'British' kingdoms of Strathclyde, Lothian and Celtic Dalriada (Argyll) had emerged and Scotland, as one nation, began to take shape in the time of King Kenneth MacAlpin.

Some chiefs claimed descent from

ancient kings which may not have been accurate in every case.

By the twelfth and thirteenth centuries the clans and families were more strongly brought under the central control of Scottish monarchs.

Lands were awarded and administered more and more under royal favour, yet the power of the area clan chiefs was still very great.

The long wars to ensure Scotland's independence against the expansionist ideas of English monarchs extended the influence of some clans and reduced the lands of others.

Those who supported Scotland's greatest king, Robert the Bruce, were awarded the territories of the families who had opposed his claim to the Scottish throne.

In the Scottish Borders country - the notorious Debatable Lands - the great families built up a ferocious reputation for providing war-like men accustomed to raiding into England and occasionally fighting one another.

Chiefs had the power to dispense justice

and to confiscate lands and clan warfare produced a society where martial virtues - courage,
hardiness, tenacity - were greatly admired.

Gradually the relationship between the
clans and the Crown became strained as Scottish
monarchs became more orientated to life in the
Lowlands and, on occasion, towards England.

The Highland clans spoke a different language, Gaelic, whereas the language of Lowland
Scotland and the court was Scots and in more
modern times, English.

Highlanders dressed differently, had different customs, and their wild mountain land
sometimes seemed almost foreign to people liv-
ing in the Lowlands.

It must be emphasised that Gaelic culture
was very rich and story-telling, poetry, piping, the
clarsach (harp) and other music all flourished and
were greatly respected.

Highland culture was different from
other parts of Scotland but it was not inferior or
less sophisticated.

Central Government, whether in London

*Clan warfare produced a society where courage
and tenacity were greatly admired.*

or Edinburgh, sometimes saw the Gaelic clans as a challenge to their authority and some sent expeditions into the Highlands and west to crush the power of the Lords of the Isles.

Nevertheless, when the eighteenth century Jacobite Risings came along the cause of the Stuarts was mainly supported by Highland clans.

The word Jacobite comes from the Latin for James - Jacobus. The Jacobites wanted to restore the exiled Stuarts to the throne of Britain.

The monarchies of Scotland and England became one in 1603 when King James VI of Scotland (1st of England) gained the English throne after Queen Elizabeth died.

The Union of Parliaments of Scotland and England, the Treaty of Union, took place in 1707.

Some Highland clans, of course, and Lowland families opposed the Jacobites and supported the incoming Hanoverians.

After the Jacobite cause finally went down at Culloden in 1746 a kind of ethnic cleansing took place. The power of the chiefs was curtailed. Tartan and the pipes were banned in law.

Many emigrated, some because they wanted to, some because they were evicted by force. In addition, many Highlanders left for the cities of the south to seek work.

Many of the clan lands became home to sheep and deer shooting estates.

But the warlike traditions of the clans and the great Lowland and Border families lived on, with their descendants fighting bravely for freedom in two world wars.

Remember the men from whence you came, says the Gaelic proverb, and to that could be added the role of many heroic women.

The spirit of the clan, of having roots, whether Highland or Lowland, means much to thousands of people.

Chapter two:

Torched and Massacred

The story of the famous Borders family, the Douglases, is so closely interwoven with that of the Scottish throne and the momentous events which shaped Scotland's story you could easily be forgiven for thinking that the Douglas line were kings in their own right.

Although the family are today primarily identified as a Borders outfit, Dubh-glas is a Gaelic phrase which means 'black stream' and it seems likely that the Douglases took their name from such a stream in Lanarkshire.

Although the earliest family history is obscured by the mists of time, Theobaldus Flammaticus or Theobold the Fleming is almost certainly the progenitor of the Douglas dynasty having, in 1147, received lands by the Douglas Water in Lanarkshire in return for services performed for the Abbot of Kelso.

By 1179 William de Douglas was in place

and we find him signing charters up till 1213. It seems likely that he was Theobold's son and heir and is the first to have taken the Douglas name.

Flourishing thereabouts in the late 1200s was another William Douglas nicknamed 'Le Hardi' because of his bold and chivalrous exploits, being the first Scots nobleman to to have risen up in support of William Wallace as he struggled to overthrow English occupation of Scotland. The English king, Edward I, had Le Hardi locked up and awarded his castle and lands to one of his own knights.

On to the scene at this juncture trots arguably the most famous of all the legion of Douglases and one of the most charismatic characters in the crowded pages of Scots history – William's son, Sir James, a cohort of the patriot king, Robert the Bruce.

The recapture by Sir James (1286-1330) of the family seat led to an incident which has become known to history as the affair of the 'Douglas Larder'. When he eventually stormed the castle of Douglas, James then proceeded to destroy his own property, putting all the buildings

to the torch, slaying the garrison and throwing their bodies along with the castle's salt supply and the contents of the wine cellar into the well to render the fortress unusable.

This bloody incident was only the first in a series of dramatic episodes in which Sir James features as a freedom fighter. During the Wars of Independence which saw Scotland secure its freedom from England, Sir James was considered by most contemporary observers to be Bruce's most ardent and skilled commander.

In the run up to Bannockburn the recovery of Roxburgh Castle in 1313 added greatly to his reputation as a military strategist and imaginative thinker and for centuries this incident was recalled as one of the most romantic incidents of the Wars.

In the half-light of dusk Sir James's men crawled forward through a herd of black cattle blending into the scene under their black cloaks until they were directly under the castle walls.

Before the garrison realised they had been duped the Scots scaled the battlements and took control, the battle cry 'A Douglas A Douglas' ringing round the fortress. Strategically this was a crucial success helping regain Teviotdale, an important gateway to Scotland, for Bruce and at the same time striking a telling psychological blow in the overall campaign.

But surely Sir James's most famous exploit came in an attempt to fulfil a vow of Robert the Bruce to make a pilgrimage to the Holy Land. When Bruce died in 1329 Douglas took the king's embalmed heart with him on a crusade.

En route, in the South of Spain where the Christian forces were struggling to drive the Moslems back to North Africa, he joined the campaign and was feted as one of Europe's greatest knights. However, near the castle of Teba in Andalusia, he was killed.

Every Scots schoolchild used to know the story of how Douglas, seeing all avenues of escape sealed off, threw the precious casket into the fray and charged after it to his death. Bruce's heart was recovered and buried in Melrose Abbey where, in its leaded container, it was unearthed and subjected to scientific tests in 1996.

Douglas himself, known to history as the 'Good Sir James' was returned to Scotland for burial in St Bride's Kirk in his native valley of Douglas.

By the Middle Ages the Douglas family had blossomed into two distinctive lines, the Black and the Red Douglases. Good Sir James was the first to carry the cognomen of the Black Douglas, supposedly because of his swarthy complexion, while the other branch gave rise to the line of the Red Douglases, the Earls of Angus, so-called because of their ruddy complexions and/or their red hair.

The adventures of both these important houses have been significant in Scottish history and they could, just occasionally, find themselves in opposing camps.

Sir James's nephew William became the first Earl of Douglas during the reign of David II (1329-1371) and by marriage added the Earldom of Mar to the family's possessions. His son, another James, the Second Earl, was the hero of the Battle of Otterburn (1388), the individual whose death in the conflict was kept from his troops as they fought, thereby securing victory over Henry Percy, 'Hotspur', son of the Earl of Northumberland. This particular Douglas has become known by the strange memorial – 'The Dead Man who won a Battle'.

The Third Earl, 'Archibald the Grim', is not remembered for his exploits on the battle-field but for his skills as a diplomatist, cleverly contriving the development of the family through strategic marriages which greatly increased the Douglases already vast estates. Two of his children married into the royal family.

At the height of their influence the Douglas family held most of the Southwest of Scotland and could call on a force of tens of thousands when their cause seemed endangered. Naturally, this almost regal power caused jealousy and anxiety not only among the noble families but even in the royal councils.

Bearing this in mind, the next Earl of Douglas who is encountered is exceptional. He was Archibald, nicknamed the 'Tyneman' or 'Loser'. At the Battle of Homildon Hill (1402), he failed to sanction a cavalry charge and the Scots were defeated, Douglas being wounded and captured by Hotspur. He then joined his captor against the English king Henry and was again taken prisoner this time at Shrewsbury. His contribution to these historic events earned him a place in Shakespeare's Henry IV.

Gathering a force of 10,000 Scots we next find him setting off for France to help in the campaign against the English where he received the singular honour of being appointed Lieutenant General of the French forces – a pointer to the solidity of the Auld Alliance at this particular period. At the same time he was given the prestigious title of Duke of Touraine.

Maintaining the family's strong ties with the power bases in Scotland the 'Tyneman' had married Margaret, a daughter of Robert III, but fighting in the French cause he was killed at the Battle of Verneuil (1424), when with John, Earl of Buchan as his co-commander the Scots were defeated by an English army under the Duke of Bedford.

Chapter three:

The Black Dinner

When the Douglases were among the great powerbrokers of Medieval Scotland it was inevitable that their own story would be tinged with tragedy as well as triumph. Of all the many tales concerning the clan, perhaps the saga of the 'Black Dinner' at Edinburgh Castle which concerns the 'Tyneman's' grandson William, the handsome, teenage Sixth Earl of Douglas, is the most heart rending and gory.

James II was still a minor and the Regency was being shared between Sir William Crichton, the chancellor of Scotland and Livingston of Callendar, Governor of Edinburgh Castle. These men feared that their influence at the court would evaporate once the personable young Douglas grew to a man. They were determined to seize the moment and take control of events.

William and his younger brother David with a youthful attendant Malcolm Fleming of Cumbernauld were wined and dined at the castle and it seems that the young king was delighted to have struck up a friendship with youths nearer his own age, rather than the old men who surrounded him.

However, at the conclusion of the dinner the head of a black bull on a salver was placed in front of the boys. Although the young Earl demanded to know the meaning of this act, the more senior members of the company knew that a death sentence had been passed on the Douglas boys. The three youths were hustled into the courtyard to be beheaded with the minimum of ceremony and the king pleading vainly for mercy on their behalf. In his last act William asked that his younger brother be executed first to spare him the horror of watching the sword fall. Terrible times indeed.

Gluttony was a rare vice in Medieval Scotland where starvation was a more common experience but the executed William's successor

James the Gross had one claim to fame. On his death in 1443 he was found to have four stones of tallow in his stomach.

Twelve years after the dreadful dinner at Edinburgh the Douglases once again found themselves spectacularly in the spotlight – this time James II taking the initiative himself in dealing a substantial, if unpremediated blow against the Douglases.

In no way had the atrocious execution of the boys diminished the power of the family. The Eighth Earl, another William, shared much of the administration of the kingdom with James II but perhaps, quite naturally, the king began to grow jealous of Douglas's power. When the Earl signed a pact of mutual protection with a group of other influential noblemen including the Earl of Ross and the Earl of Crawford, (only recently in revolt against the king) that was too much for James who sensed rebellion in the air.

Once more the power of the family had reached a dangerous level. One commentator suggested that they were so numerous and wielded such power and potency – 'that the king reigned but by their licence and courtesy, as it were'.

Under promise of safe conduct the Earl was invited to Stirling Castle. When Douglas refused to go back on the pact with Crawford and Co., James flew into a rage, a characteristic of this fiery monarch, and stabbed Douglas. Medical records show that his body carried 26 clearly identifiable knife wounds.

After this event the power of the Douglases was soon restricted. William's young brother James declared against the Scottish king but the monarch was not going to miss his chance and in March, 1455, James attacked the Douglas stronghold at Inveravon near Linlithgow. By this time James Douglas was in open rebellion having pinned a notice renouncing his allegiance to the door of Parliament House... but the game was up.

The King demolished Inveravon and marched into the Borders. Douglas remained defiant but his army, sensing a dramatic downturn in the family fortunes, began to drift away. James eventually fled to England and in a last stand at Arkinholm near Langholm in May, 1455, his brothers were defeated by royal forces. Effectively it was the end of the road for the Black Douglases. James died in a monastic retreat.

In a remarkable twist, however, it also meant a fresh beginning for that other branch of the family, the Red Douglases. The Fourth Douglas Earl of Angus, George (d. 1462) profited by the fall of his kinsfolk and was, in fact, in command of the royal forces at Arkinholm.

Chapter four:

'Bell the Cat'

Of the Red Douglas Earls of Angus, Archibald, the fifth Earl (1449-1513) is certainly the best known to history from his nickname 'Bell the Cat'.

He led a conspiracy against Robert Cochrane, stonemason and architectural favourite of James III, telling the fable about the brave mouse who was prepared to tie a bell around the sleeping cat's neck so that others would be warned of the feline approach.

At the national disaster at the Battle of Flodden two of Archibald's sons were killed along with 200 members of the Douglas clan.

As the Medieval period came to a close the Red Douglases found themselves, like their Black Douglas predecessors, envied for their wealth and power. But on to this scene in the late 1400s came a man who took the family in an unexpected direction – Gavin Douglas, a son of

Bell-the-Cat, a poet-cleric who achieved great literary distinction with his magnum opus, a translation of Virgil's *Aeneid* into the Scots tongue.

Gavin Douglas's ecclesiastical career was less impressive than his literary fortunes. By 1503 he was provost of the Collegiate Church of St Giles in Edinburgh and was nominated to the archbishopric of St Andrews in 1514 without success; the following year he was Bishop of Dunkeld and he died in London in 1522 from the plague, still trying to persuade Cardinal Wolsey to support his claim to the archbishopric of St Andrews. In the Douglas tradition he was a master plotter and intriguer.

Very few of his poems survive. His fame, say his biographers, rest on the Virgil translation, thirteen volumes each with a prologue in which among other diversions Douglas touched on the Scottish weather. He was an 'assured' poet with a feeling for landscape and man's joys and sufferings.

In keeping with the Douglas habit of ending up on the top of the pile Bell-the-Cat was succeeded by his grandson, also Archibald, the Sixth 'Red' Earl who married Margaret Tudor, the widow of James IV killed at Flodden.

He played an unpredictable role in Scottish affairs and from 1525 kept James V prisoner and dominated the country. When the king escaped Angus fled to England but returned to lead the Scots to victory at Ancrum Moor (1545) and had a share in the defeat at the Battle of Pinkie, as Scotland resisted English attempts to force a marriage between Mary, Queen of Scots and Prince Edward – the 'Rough Wooing'.

While the high heid yins in the family politicked and plotted other less well-known Douglases were at work almost out of sight of history. In this period when Mary was deposed and imprisoned Archibald Douglas, 'parson of Glasgow', who was Lord of Session in 1565 was said to have been involved in the murders of Riccio, the Queen's favourite (1566) and that of Lord Darnley, a Douglas too you'll recall, at Kirk o' Field in Edinburgh (1567). James VI pardoned his support of Mary in 1586.

Other Douglases who had their moment in the sun include Katherine Douglas remembered for delaying the assassins of James I at Perth by thrusting her arm through the staples of a door at the Dominican Friary; Willie and George Douglas of Lochleven who helped Mary, Queen of Scots flee her island prison; and Wigtownshire's William Douglas, a pedlar who made his fortune in the Virginian trade in the 1700s and had Castle Douglas raised to burgh status.

Archibald, Eighth Earl of Douglas, is considered the last of the true Red Douglases. Elsewhere, James Douglas, Lord of Dalkeith, was created Lord of Morton, and yet another powerful branch of the Douglases came into play. The fourth Earl of Morton, also James was a committed Reformer who was Regent of Scotland from 1572-1578 but paid with his life for his role in the murder of Lord Darnley.

The Angus title passed to William Douglas of Glenbervie and the Morton earldom to Douglas of Lochleven and although the memorable days when the family was feared throughout the land were no more the Douglases still seemed to be able to accumulate titles and add the Queensberry Home and Selkirk lines.

By 1703 the Angus line were the Dukes of Douglas and the scene was set for perhaps the family's most keenly fought and intriguing encounter in five hundred years. The battlefield was an Edinburgh courtroom.

This event followed the death of the childless first Duke in 1761 and has become known to history as the 'Douglas Cause'.

Claims to his estate by his nephew Archibald James Edward Douglas were contested by the Duke of Hamilton, Lord Douglas Hamilton and Sir Hew Dalrymple. In the first instance the Court of Session decided, on the casting vote of the Lord President, against young Archie but the verdict was reversed by the House of Lords eight years later. This decision was greeted by public rejoicing in Edinburgh with 'the windows of the capital illuminated' and those of the ,judges who had found against the popular young man being the target for stone throwers.

Chapter five:

World of Achievement

Away from the intrigues of court and the politics of the Scottish nation, the Douglases have consistently figured in the shaping of events both at home and abroad in the past two centuries.

One of the most colourful characters to carry the Douglas handle was Scone-born postman's son and botanist David Douglas after whom the Oregon pine (and a North American squirrel) is named.

After learning his trade as a gardener in Perthshire and at Glasgow's Botanic Gardens he began a series of epic botanical expeditions to North America to collect plants. His efforts were widely recognised and he soon found himself commissioned to make an extended tour of the Americas, concluding with a triumphant return to the United Kingdom.

He was responsible for the discovery of a

wide range of trees, shrubs and herbaceous plants, some 200 of which he introduced to the United Kingdom and which are today found widely across the country.

This adventurer who trekked across thousands of miles of the American wilderness was always unlikely to die a clean, in-between-the-sheets death but his end was spectacular even by the standards of 19th century explorers. While on another botanic journey, this time to the Hawaiian Islands, he tripped and fell into a pit which had been dug to trap a wild bull and was gored to death by the cornered beast.

In America's pioneering days we find Douglas doctors working in the Colonies; Frederick Lloyd, a Negro fugitive adopted the surname Douglass as he campaigned against slavery after escaping from a Baltimore shipyard and his name became known around the world; Stephen Douglas from Vermont was nominated for the US presidency in 1860 but was defeated by Abraham Lincoln; and out on the wild frontier of Arizona, immigrants like Jimmy Douglass, born on board ship in the early 1800s, contested for years with the Apache for the right to farm on the Santa Cruz Valley. His Sopori ranch was often under attack in the 1850s but this determined Douglas was there to stay.

There was a Douglas Governor of New Brunswick in Canada, a Sir Robert Douglas who was one of Europe's leading experts on China in the 1870s, and Austrian born Norman Douglas is remembered for his natural history sketches and his baffling novels.

In the Antipodes Sir Adye Douglas was premier of Tasmania while across the Tasman Sea John Douglas from Perthshire was a pioneer of New Zealand's frozen meat industry.

From their humble beginnings beside the Douglas Water this illustrious – and now enormous – Scottish family have spread themselves around the globe with a record of achievement which justifies the clan motto – Jamais Arrièrre (Never Behind).